Directing Agile Change

Association for Project Management

Association for Project Management
Ibis House, Regent Park
Summerleys Road, Princes Risborough
Buckinghamshire
HP27 9LE

© Association for Project Management 2016

All rights reserved. No part of this publication may be reproduced, stored in a retrieval system, or transmitted, in any form or by any means, without the express permission in writing of the Association for Project Management. Within the UK exceptions are allowed in respect of any fair dealing for the purposes of research or private study, or criticism or review, as permitted under the Copyright, Designs and Patents Act, 1988, or in the case of reprographic reproduction in accordance with the terms of the licences issued by the Copyright Licensing Agency. Enquiries concerning reproduction outside these terms and in other countries should be sent to the Rights Department, Association for Project Management at the address above.

British Library Cataloguing in Publication Data is available.
Paperback ISBN: 978-1-903494-60-8
eISBN: 978-1-903494-61-5

Cover design by Fountainhead Creative Consultants
Typeset by RefineCatch Limited, Bungay, Suffolk
in 11/14 pt Foundry Sans

Contents

Figures and tables   iv
Foreword   v
Acknowledgements   vi

1   Context and introduction   1
    1.1   Agile   1
    1.2   Research   2
    1.3   Using agile   3
    1.4   Agile development methods   3
    1.5   Agile myths   4

2   Principles of agile governance   7
    2.1   Introduction   7
    2.2   Good governance principles   8
    2.3   Principles for governance of agile change   8

3   When to adopt an agile approach   11
    3.1   Introduction   11
    3.2   The options   11

4   Gaining value from agile   15
    4.1   Portfolio direction   15
    4.2   Implementation of agile approaches across the enterprise   15
    4.3   Key governance roles and accountability   16
    4.4   Disclosure and reporting   16
    4.5   Measurement   16
    4.6   Modified behaviours   17

5   Governance guidance lists   19
    5.1   The board (or delegated sub-committee)   19
    5.2   Project sponsor   20
    5.3   Project manager   22
    5.4   External reviewer   23

Appendix A: References and further information   25
Appendix B: Compendium of agile development methods   26

Figures and tables

Figures

1.1	Key differences in approach and concept from traditional project management	2
1.2	Chaos Manifesto output	2
2.1	Waterfall versus agile process summary	8
3.1	Spectrum of application	12

Tables

1.1	Myths about agile governance	4
2.1	Principles for governance of agile change	9
3.1	Differences between agile and traditional project management approaches	12

Foreword

Agile working is increasingly recognised by organisations as a competitive advantage, where a speedier but controlled response is needed to changing environmental conditions. How should organisations oversee the delivery of agile projects? This guide provides the answer.

Global brands such as Amazon and Apple have agility at the core of their business model. Transforming an entire organisation to be 'agile' may not always be either practical or sensible. However, delivering change projects by using agile approaches is likely to return significant value to the organisation.

There is a need for a different governance response to match agile approaches. Some proponents suggest that agile avoids the need for discipline, documentation and governance. This guide strongly suggests the opposite but that some adaptation to governance and focus on collaborative behaviours is necessary.

The guide is aimed at those involved in the governance of all change initiatives. Whether organised as projects, programmes or portfolios of change. It has an emphasis on those that sit at the apex of governance, i.e. board members, sponsors and external reviewers. It lists principles and check lists that directors and their equivalents should adopt and questions that you should ask. It will help improve your corporate performance, motivate staff, reduce shocks at boardroom level, safeguard your reputation and avoid hardship to stakeholders.

This guide explains how good governance of agile projects is enabled and primarily suggests an adapted mindset and collaborative behaviours that can be:

- applied at any level of leadership in the organisation from the main board/chief executive level downwards;
- combined with any of the popular agile methods;
- shared throughout an organisation to encourage more successful strategic investments and further technical innovation.

Jennifer Stapleton
Agile management evangelist

Acknowledgements

The authors of this document are Brian Wernham, Adrian Pyne, Roger Garrini and Martin Samphire. The guide was written in conjunction with the APM Governance Specific Interest Group (SIG).

The authors and APM would like to thank the following for taking the time to review and comment on early drafts of this publication: Mark Rackham, Keith Richards and Darren Wilmhurst, as well as the SIG committee members and reader reviewers.

1

Context and introduction

1.1 Agile

"Agile is a state of mind", says Steve Messenger, chair, DSDM Consortium (see Appendix B).

'Being agile' requires new behaviours as well as different procedures:

- within projects and/or programmes (referred to hereafter as 'projects');
- across the organisational environment of projects (referred to hereafter as 'enterprise project management').

At the core of agile is the requirement to exhibit core values and behaviours of trust, flexibility, empowerment and collaboration.

Collaboration rather than confrontation is the focus in the agile approach. Traditional 'waterfall' project management approaches seek to capture up front the detailed requirements for a product or service, put it into a contract-like specification and then assume that little will change. Agile recognises that user needs and the environment into which projects are delivered change. Agile builds in from the outset the ability to change priorities and elaborate requirements as more is understood about the service or product. Sometimes a 'hybrid' approach can be used with some activities being 'agile', and some being 'waterfall'.

Traditional planning assumes that few changes of course will be required from inception to completion. But where innovation is required and uncertainty exists, then changes of 'tack' may frequently be needed. Some elements of a programme may be more certain than others, in which case a 'hybrid' approach may be optimal. These differences in approach are illustrated in Figure 1.1.

Good governance of project management is described in the APM guide *Directing Change*, which should be read alongside this guide. To avoid repetition, throughout this guide, the word project will mean equally project, programme or portfolio as explained in *APM Body of Knowledge*.

Directing Agile Change

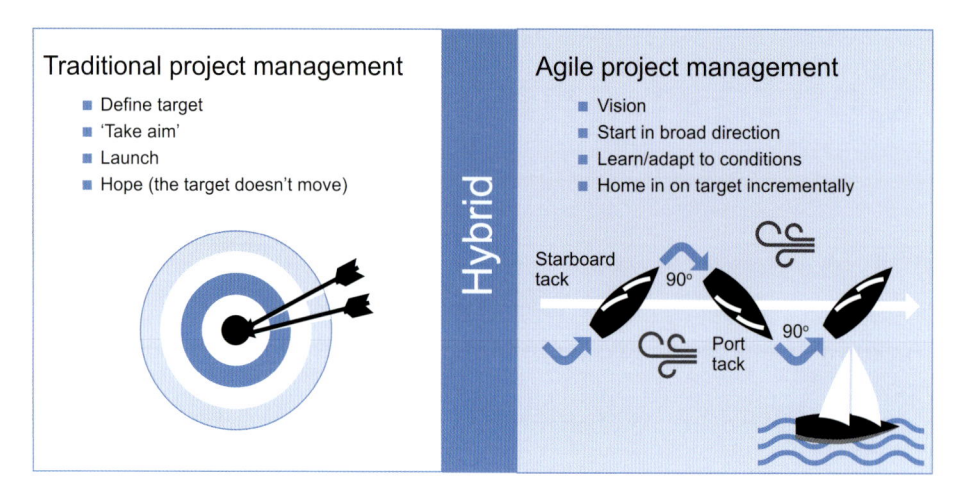

Figure 1.1 Key differences in approach and concept from traditional project management

1.2 Research

The Standish Group released an annual report called the *Chaos Manifesto*. Its 2012 report stated that agile projects succeed three times as often as waterfall projects (see Figure 1.2).

Notice that there was no significant change in the percentage of 'challenged' projects between categories.

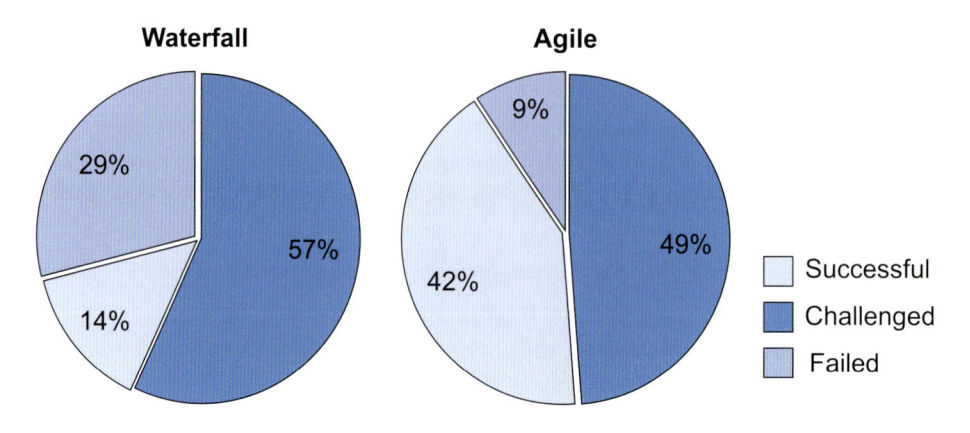

Figure 1.2 Chaos Manifesto output

APM research into the *Conditions for Project Success*, has similarly found that smaller, shorter projects had a significantly higher success rate than bigger, longer ones.

1.3 Using agile

Sometimes a traditional approach will be optimal. Agile works where the business requirement has cost and time parameters that are 'hard' and the prioritised scope and benefits are 'soft'. Agile project management focuses on delivering maximum value against business priorities in the time and budget allowed. Lessons are learned from the feedback from practical implementation. Good project management disciplines are still applied, irrespective of whether agile, waterfall or a hybrid approach is adopted.

How much time should be spent upfront in a project developing appropriate delivery strategies and plans? We take the view that 'just enough' (to avoid near term nugatory work) strategy, architecture and planning work should take place before starting development activities.

Agile may present other challenges to an enterprise including:

- having a consistent method for incremental delivery at the heartbeat of the business, not at the convenience of the project team;
- evolving solutions with stakeholders;
- building teams with accountability and authority to benefit the business;
- maintaining alignment of development activities and product releases with strategic business objectives.

Here we focus on the governance of agile projects not agile development methods with a set of principles and behaviours that will facilitate any of the major popular 'agile' methods.

1.4 Agile development methods

Agile working is not limited to software development, but can also be applied to many aspects of an organisation. A list of common agile development methods that claim to follow the Agile Manifesto are summarised in Appendix B.

1.5 Agile myths

Table 1.1 Myths about agile governance

Myth	Reality
Agile is only for stars.	Agile working produces best value when there are capable agile project teams, operating in a supportive agile landscape. To gain value from agile governance, organisations need to invest in it.
Agile does not fit our culture.	Where there is an unshakeable, controlling, centralised culture this is true. However, many organisations manage to adapt their culture and procedures to create an agile landscape.
Agile only works for small projects.	While individual agile teams tend to be effective when small, good behaviour can scale up to the overall delivery team.
Agile requires co-location.	Agile working does emphasise the value of face-to-face working. However, web-based collaboration tools, use of internal social media, combined with strong agile leadership, can encourage highly effective distributed agile teams. We consider that face-to-face is most effective.
We don't need a business case.	Incorrect – being agile stresses the need to maximise delivery of value against a set budget and/or timescale.
Agile lacks project management processes and documentation.	Incorrect – agile working has structure and discipline, it is just different from traditional project management processes. Key documents are still needed for communication.
We don't need to produce documentation on agile projects.	Incorrect – appropriate documentation is still needed as part of the project management discipline, communication and for recording core data.
Our organisation's individual accountability systems don't fit agile.	Probably true, but they can be adapted to agile working; e.g. include sponsorship responsibilities in the purpose and objectives of executives who are named as sponsors.
Agile is just a fad.	Unlikely – working in this way has in fact existed for many years, albeit not with the agile tag or with such intensity.
There are better ideas than agile.	Possibly – an agile approach needs to be applied only where it adds value and is more effective than traditional approaches.

Table 1.1 *Continued*

Myth	Reality
You cannot mix agile and traditional approaches.	Incorrect – agile governance and agile project management can be adapted to both agile and non-agile delivery activity, or a mixture of both.
Agile is better than traditional approaches.	Incorrect – agile is more appropriate in some circumstances and should be avoided in others.
Agile is just another mechanistic method.	The managers' mindset needed is different from traditional waterfall approaches. 'Being agile' is much more about the journey than the destination.
Agile is for software development.	Although the term gained currency in software development, agile working has existed in business-wide use for some time, albeit not tagged 'agile'. Agile is applicable for business use across an enterprise, although there is a language that can mystify the use of agile.
Scrum is an agile project management method.	Incorrect – Scrum is a well-oriented technique for managing a team dealing with a backlog of work, but it lacks the project management 'wrapper'.
Existing decision-making processes can deal with agile projects.	Unlikely – many senior decision making bodies (investment boards, etc.) occur at fixed dates (e.g. monthly). For agile projects, senior governance meetings or decisions need to be driven by project timescales/needs, not by the business drum beat. Therefore, such bodies may need to meet irregularly and more often, driven by the requirements of the projects. Also many decisions that have been traditionally made at senior levels are delegated down to lower levels.

2

Principles of agile governance

2.1 Introduction

Good governance is about selecting an approach for each project that maximises the chances of a successful outcome.

Agile divides up otherwise unwieldly, large, long-term projects into smaller increments of product delivery that are at a 'cadence' that reflects the heartbeat of the business. These increments are further broken down into 'timeboxes' (sometimes called 'sprints'), which match the natural (usually shorter) timescales for each step of technical development.

Agile allows for activities and outputs to evolve without the need to create an over-detailed definition of the final output before the requirements and the possible solutions have been fully explored. Agile accepts that the best final result will emerge based upon incremental outputs, review and feedback, at speed. The approach aims to ensure that changes from a dynamic project environment are routinely built into the evolving project roadmap.

With an agile approach a useable product is delivered in incremental steps, building increasing capability and thus building confidence with the business.

Agile can be scaled up to large projects or programmes, for example by having multiple sub-projects, creating tranches of projects, etc.

Sometimes the delivery approach may mix both agile and waterfall projects, and in this respect all delivery does not have to be iterative. Some parts may take a traditional approach, e.g. construction of a new building.

Directing Agile Change

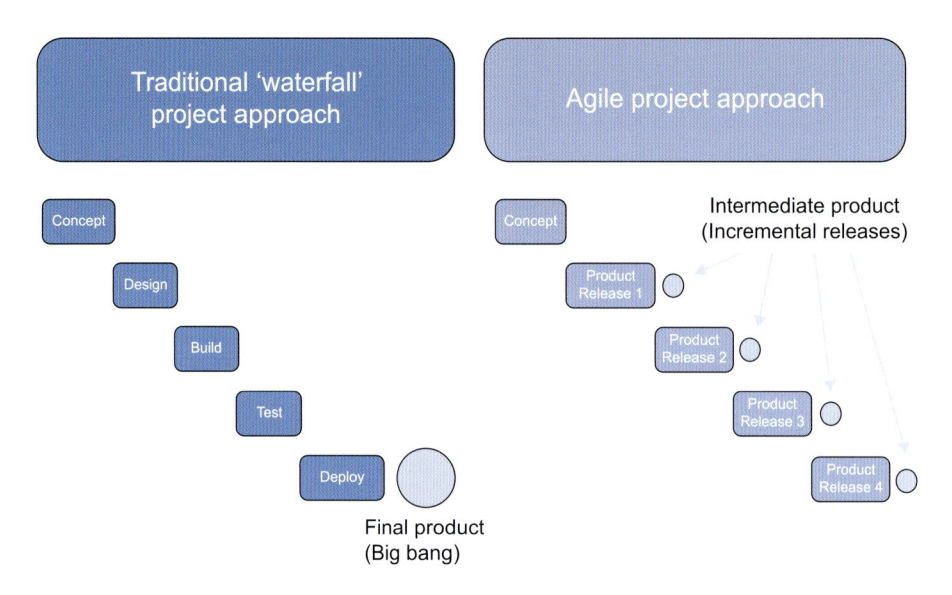

Figure 2.1 Waterfall versus agile process summary

2.2 Good governance principles

Good governance principles are explained in the sister publications to this guide, *Directing Change* and *Sponsoring Change*.

2.3 Principles for governance of agile change

The following principles for governance of agile projects are additional to those listed in *Directing Change*.

Principles of agile governance

Table 2.1 Principles for governance of agile change

No.	Principle	Explanation
1	*Focus on the business need*	Benefits are prioritised and are realised incrementally. The most valued and key features are developed in the early releases: lower value ones are left to later releases – often it becomes evident that they are of poor value/not required and costs can be saved.
2	*Value driven*	Focusing on delivering the maximum value within a fixed time period or budget. The desired benefits are prioritised and are delivered according to that priority.
3	*Incremental delivery*	Visible products are delivered incrementally as releases of capability (something that can be seen working). An overall 'roadmap' is produced to show the strategic direction. Just enough detailed planning is done upfront of each phase or 'sprint', but with only high level planning produced for the later releases (rolling wave planning).
4	*Timebox delivery*	Each 'sprint' or release is timeboxed. Delivery on time is mandated. Of the individual release variables, time (and cost) are fixed, but scope and benefits can be flexed.
5	*Empowered teams and decision making*	Decision making is delegated to the lowest possible level so that decisions can be made, at speed, to still meet the next milestone. People are empowered to take quick decisions that they feel would most benefit the product, team and the business. Senior governance meetings or decisions are driven by project needs, not by business drumbeat.
6	*Collaboration*	A collaborative approach is essential – a 'one team' approach. Co-location of the entire team is advantageous. An atmosphere of trust and honesty is observed within the team. Teams celebrate achievements often.
7	*Enhanced communication*	Communication is rapid and effective – daily 'stand-up' meetings help to resolve issues rapidly. There is early and on-going close involvement of the product owner and senior user(s) to enhance understanding, validate the solution and create next steps.
8	*Just enough definition*	Initial definition is kept high-level. There is a clear and transparent mechanism to incorporate changes to requirements. Unnecessary changes are reduced to avoid distracting the delivery team. Just enough is delivered to satisfy the vision.

(Continued)

Table 2.1 Continued

No.	Principle	Explanation
9	Constant striving for improvement	An agile capability is built in the organisation where people are expected to challenge and continuously improve, and learn and embed lessons from each phase or sprint.
10	'Learn forward'	If a project becomes non-viable, it is 'failed' early. From a portfolio view this may mean failing often and learning quickly to produce success.
11	Demonstrate control	Transparent, clear and rapid reporting to stakeholders using facts and evidence. Progress is measured through the delivery of products and benefits rather than completed activities.
12	Change control	Embrace change that enhances value. Changes to requirements and scope that enhances value are embraced – these are rigorously reviewed, approved or rejected, prioritised, registered and subsequently inputted into the individual project or releases. Major changes are not attempted within a live project or release.

3

When to adopt an agile approach

3.1 Introduction

A critical governance decision is to select the appropriate approach as part of the project strategy. An agile approach, when used in an appropriate context, and supported by top management within a supportive framework, can produce excellent results. However, an agile approach may also fail if used in an inappropriate context.

There is a spectrum of options that might be chosen for a particular situation. PRINCE2 Agile® and DSDM has an 'agilometer' to enable you to assess the risk and benefit of using or not using agile. In Figure 3.1 we outline, by way of example, projects where the agile approach might be most suitably applied.

3.2 The options

Figure 3.1 lists some characteristics that should be considered before selecting which approach might be most suitable. Exploring each of the characteristics should give the governance/decision makers a good pointer towards the appropriate direction.

A hybrid will consist of both agile and traditional components, and may be useful for larger scale change, e.g. a programme, where some projects will use iterative delivery, and others require serial delivery. An example of this may be the iterative delivery of a new IT system, but with a serial roll-out project at multiple sites. The whole programme can still be managed in an agile way; the delivery approach of individual projects can vary, making it a hybrid.

Table 3.1 shows a number of key areas of project governance and how an agile approach differs from a traditional waterfall approach to managing projects.

Directing Agile Change

| Waterfall | Hybrid | Agile/incremental |

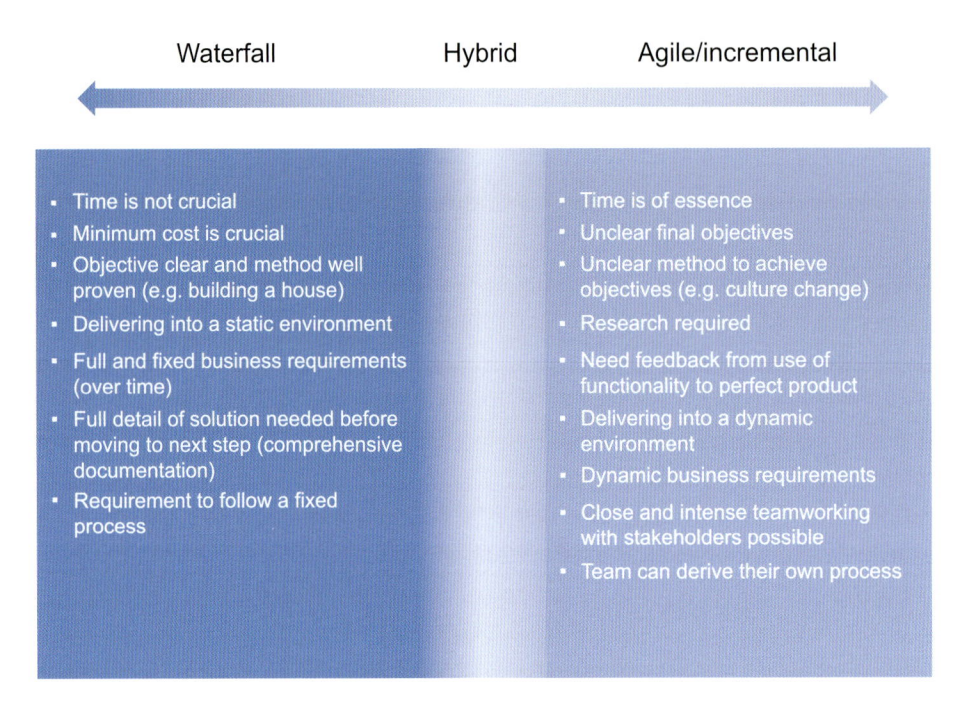

- Time is not crucial
- Minimum cost is crucial
- Objective clear and method well proven (e.g. building a house)
- Delivering into a static environment
- Full and fixed business requirements (over time)
- Full detail of solution needed before moving to next step (comprehensive documentation)
- Requirement to follow a fixed process

- Time is of essence
- Unclear final objectives
- Unclear method to achieve objectives (e.g. culture change)
- Research required
- Need feedback from use of functionality to perfect product
- Delivering into a dynamic environment
- Dynamic business requirements
- Close and intense teamworking with stakeholders possible
- Team can derive their own process

Figure 3.1 Spectrum of application

Table 3.1 Differences between agile and traditional project management approaches

Traditional	Factors	Agile
Tends to be top-down directive leadership	Leadership	Tends to be more facilitative leadership
Centralised	Control	De-centralised
Hierarchical	Decision making	Delegated and team based
Learnings captured at end Intolerance to mistakes	Learning	Continuous improvement and learning through testing/using Tolerance of mistakes where lessons learnt
On outputs at each stage	Focus during project delivery	On incremental delivery of outcomes and prioritised value/benefits at each release date (timebox)

Table 3.1 Continued

Traditional	Factors	Agile
Some staff part time alongside other projects	Resourcing	Dedicated staff in close knit teams
Directed	Team operation	Self-organising and collaborative – rigorous engagement
Driven by standard business meeting timetable	Business control	Driven by project need
Scope and functionality tends to be fixed	Objectives	Time and/or cost tend to be fixed and concentration is on providing early value
Dealt within project deliverable via change control	Major changes to outputs	Change can and should be accommodated on a value-prioritised basis. However, major change may be best dealt with outside the current release and included in subsequent releases of the product
Assumed to be predictable – narrow range of options desired	End outcome	Evolving – range of outcomes allowed
Progress to time, cost, quality	Performance measurement	Delivery of actual outputs and enablement/delivery of prioritised benefits
Guided by agreed terms of reference	Strategic guidance	Focused by the vision

4

Gaining value from agile

4.1 Portfolio direction

A key feature of agile working is managing the 'backlog'. In this, a rolling set of features are prioritised and releases of features are clustered together in an optimal manner.

The overall portfolio must still be reviewed regularly against business needs. Agile projects are designed to deliver rapidly, yet accommodate changes to portfolio priorities.

4.2 Implementation of agile approaches across the enterprise

A common criticism of agile working is that it is only successful when you have a team of agile experts. Nonetheless, an agile capability and culture need to be developed and must be actively sustained for best results.

Components of a sustained agile approach include:

- leadership, understanding and visible commitment from the board to an agile approach and its implication;
- commitment and ensuring resource availability and engagement of people (governance, delivery and users) to engage long term in agile teams and in their counterparts outside the core teams;
- excellent collaboration;
- control, but not too close;
- a defined agile governance approach, adapting existing traditional governance approaches;
- a prioritised agile 'portfolio' (backlog, feature list);
- an agile enterprise programme management office (both to co-ordinate and also to share good practices);
- agile managers – trained and experienced;

Directing Agile Change

- active learning during and after projects, then specific feed into new ones;
- provision of agile project management training and agile coaching, e.g. of sponsors;
- an agile community of practice;
- modified reward and governance policies to reflect agile working.

Building this capability requires time and investment.

There is no 'one size fits all' to agile working, so a tick-box, conformance-oriented approach will not work. In adopting an agile culture and capability, the skilled agile leaders and teams must be able to adapt the approach to each need. Adaptability is a key agile principle.

4.3 Key governance roles and accountability

Just as demonstrated in *Directing Change*, responsibilities must be assigned and clear for an agile project to succeed. The company board, the sponsor, the project board, the project manager, stakeholders and any external assurance reviewers all have key responsibilities to support the team delivering the work. For agile projects it is important that these roles are clear and delegated appropriately with understanding on all sides.

4.4 Disclosure and reporting

Openness is an important behaviour underpinning agile; it is core to transparent and effective reporting. A key aspect of agile governance is the 'lightness' of reporting. This does not mean a lack of reporting, but looking for lean ways to ensure that management has just enough information it needs for oversight; detailed, overbearing oversight is not part of an agile culture.

4.5 Measurement

Types of agile metrics to be considered include:

- delivery progress, e.g. actual versus planned features produced;
- value, e.g. actual versus planned features against cost;

- benefits attained, e.g. mapped to delivered features, their impact and priority;
- performance, e.g. rate of feature production;
- stakeholder satisfaction;
- time to operational benefits, e.g. frequency of releases;
- agility, e.g. in terms of project performance improvement, learnings implemented.

4.6 Modified behaviours

Appropriate behaviour is required whichever agile method is used. For agile work the constraints of time (and/or cost) may be immovable, whereas scope is variable to defined limits. The sponsor's 'pet' requirement can be de-scoped as priorities change. An essential part of agile governance is to step back and re-visit the overriding objectives, and progress towards them frequently.

The key behaviours that need to be exhibited for agile projects are similar to those essential to waterfall projects – but with an enhanced focus as outlined below.

For board members

- Be role models for and (visibly) demonstrate advocacy and support for agile working and culture.
- Have a high tolerance short term to 'failure', but look to 'fail' and learn fast.
- Incentivise the correct behaviours and be forthright in picking up non-agile supporting behaviours.
- By default look for dashboard reports not detailed reports.
- Accept that project decisions may/will be outside of traditional policies/practices.
- Accept that final cost and time forecasts are only that.
- Ensure resources are properly deployed to the team.

For project sponsors

- Focus on the business vision – and relate back to it – at all times. Be clear and consistent on priorities.
- Engage with the delivery team, stakeholders and users frequently and in detail – set and manage their expectations.
- Demonstrate being the change champion and lead from the front.

Directing Agile Change

- Encourage open and robust feedback.
- By default look for dashboard reports not detailed reports.
- Be accessible for rapid escalation and resolution of issues.
- Encourage collaboration and investigate and address non-collaborative behaviours.

For project managers

- Put the customer/business user at the centre of delivery.
- Manage by achievement of objectives rather than by completion of tasks.
- 'Hands off' control, close but not too close.
- Encourage collaboration and review and address non-collaborative behaviours.
- Build consensus through inclusive management.
- Be incisive and ensure decisions are made rapidly.
- Embrace uncertainty – constantly redefining and communicating release functionality.

For key point external reviewers

- Recognise that iterative delivery will require adaptation of the review points process, e.g. entry/exit criteria may be different.
- Really check business case validity and what has changed/been learned.
- Robustly challenge benefits/outcomes. Worry less about process and adherence to policy.

5
Governance guidance lists

Senior executives have asked what they should focus upon to add value in their governance roles. They often feel bamboozled with the jargon used by those immersed in an agile methodology. The intention of the checklists below is to remove the mystique and enable anyone involved in a key governance role to ask the appropriate and probing question.

The checklists are structured around the key generic governance roles. Also they assume incremental delivery for projects using an agile approach. It is down to the reader to interpret between the generic roles given below and the specifics of their organisation.

Use these checklists as a starting point in considering whether agile is appropriate. Could it be a risk? Or would a hybrid approach be better?

Again these lists should also be read alongside the checklists given in *Directing Change*, which they supplement.

5.1 The board (or delegated sub-committee)

Ref	Description
1	Have you previously consulted and acted upon the guidance within the APM guide, *Directing Change*?
	Are you clear about the visions of each project in the portfolio, business priorities and portfolio alignment, appointment of sponsors, roles and responsibilities, creation and maintenance of project management capability, success measures, disclosure and reporting? Does an overall business target operating model exist that clearly shows how benefits are accrued?
2	Do processes exist in your organisation to ensure a formal and conscious assessment of project strategy and whether agile working is appropriate?
3	Are there business cases for all projects, which are revisited formally at agreed and frequent intervals? Is there a business architect who maintains an overview of how releases contribute to enhanced performance and changes to the operating model?

(Continued)

Directing Agile Change

Table 5.1 *Continued*

Ref	Description
4	Have you created agile working rules and put in place training and governance mechanisms that support agile ways of working?
5	Are project decisions delegated to, and made at, the lowest level possible? Where board decisions are essential, is the process slick and fast? Do decision dates revolve around formal board meetings or agile project delivery requirement dates?
6	How do you and your board colleagues demonstrate that you understand agile working and the required behaviours to staff at all levels of the organisation? How do you know that key stakeholders understand the rules and behaviours?
7	Have you been trained in the required behaviours to support agile working?
8	Do you act rapidly on concerns and warnings from your operational and delivery teams regarding escalated project issues?
9	Is there a control process for releasing multiple business product deliverables from different projects into live operation in the business at the same time?
10	Are user department resources properly assigned and committed to agile projects and their business-as-usual responsibilities assigned elsewhere for the duration?
11	Is there evidence of exceptional collaboration between delivery teams and business users?
12	Do you hold project sponsors to account for performance and benefits delivery?

5.2 Project sponsor

Ref	Description
1	Do you feel your organisation board is demonstrating appropriate agile behaviours and is fully supportive of your project? Is funding in place for at least the next few tranches/releases?
2	How well is the project's vision aligned with the organisation's strategic objectives?
3	Have you articulated the vision and objectives of the project clearly to all stakeholders? Have you sought feedback to ensure they understand?
4	Have you defined and documented key governance roles and responsibilities and are they fully understood?
5	Have you established an effective and representative project steering group or project board to support you? Are they committed to project success and focused upon business needs and benefits delivery rather than solution details?

Governance guidance lists

Ref	Description
6	Has there been a formal and conscious assessment as whether agile working is appropriate? Is this assessment periodically revisited?
7	Are all projects coherent and 100 per cent focused on building incrementally to the overall vision?
8	Has the project team structured the work into a series of incrementally delivered project products with clear definition of the early deliverables/functionality and outline definition of the later deliverables? Is each deliverable timeboxed?
9	Are the desired outcomes and success criteria for each (early) project, release or stage clearly defined in terms of priority, measurement and functionality?
10	Have you stopped all work on projects/in the programme or portfolio that are no longer aligned?
11	Is there a robust review gate/release gate process in place with appropriate reviews scheduled in participants' diaries?
12	Are timeboxed delivery dates adhered to? How well is the expected functionality of solution delivered against these milestones? Has the business been able to use the functionality of solutions delivered to date and subsequently been able to deliver expected benefits?
13	Do benefits or product owners exist, do they feel accountable for benefits delivery and are capture arrangements in place? Are business benefits prioritised and does the project roadmap reflect delivery of the priority benefits early? Is there a single backlog of user requirements?
14	(At each review/release gate) are the project benefits still valid – and have they been independently validated?
15	Are sufficient quantity and competence of resources available to the project team? Are you comfortable with the performance of the project manager and have you fed back suggestions on performance improvement?
16	Are the delivery team and the key/senior users or stakeholders co-located and dedicated to the work in hand? How well do they understand and exhibit good agile working behaviours?
17	Are key decision making processes agile – delegated to the lowest level possible, slick and fast? Does the change control process clearly delineate decisions that can be made at different levels?
18	Do you have daily contact with the programme manager and active project managers? Are you available for decisions and reviews at a moment's notice?

(Continued)

Directing Agile Change

Table 5.2 *Continued*

Ref	Description
19	Are business change roles suitably allocated to ensure regular review of business readiness, business and technical architecture and adoption of solutions?
20	Are you committed to project success? Are you devoting appropriate time to your sponsor role?
21	Have you consulted the guidance in *Sponsoring Change*? Have you recognised your strengths and weaknesses in the sponsor role (and shared with your board) and taken steps to fill any gaps (support, training, coaching, etc.)?
22	Do you receive regular and informative reports of status? Do these reports cover collaboration and relationship performance/effectiveness? Do you also attend regular face-to-face meetings to receive progress updates?

5.3 Project manager

Ref	Description
1	Do you understand, and can you comprehensively describe, the vision of the project clearly to all stakeholders? Can you describe the priority of benefits (and sub-benefits) and demonstrate how these are delivered during the early projects/releases? Do all release managers likewise understand? Do you know how success will be measured?
2	Is there a project roadmap that shows how both the business and, technically, the work is structured into a series of incrementally delivered projects/product deliveries with clear definition of the early deliverables and outline definition of the later deliverables? Is this mapped to the target operating model? Are any necessary manual work arounds defined and agreed?
3	Are all projects in a programme coherent and focused on building incrementally to the overall vision? Are interfaces and interdependencies with other projects understood?
4	Are 'lessons learned' and shared as a central activity in the project/release plan? Are post project/stage lessons learned reviews carried out formally and lessons built into future projects/stages?
5	Are release managers encouraged to identify and exploit opportunities for improvements to outcomes?
6	Are the resources engaged on the project sufficiently competent for their role, using proven methods, tools and standards? Has appropriate training been given for the tasks being undertaken?

Governance guidance lists

Ref	Description
7	Are the key stage or project deliverables defined by a milestone. Is delivery timeboxed and are delivery dates held? Has the business been able to use the functionality of solutions delivered to date and subsequently been able to deliver expected benefits? Is successful achievement of milestones celebrated?
8	Is the business and technical architecture reviewed frequently, updated, communicated and revisions built into the later project/stage definitions?
9	Are agreements in place to support live operation? Do they stress collaboration rather than being adversarial contracts? Is there a clear strategy for exiting existing contractual arrangements where necessary?
10	Is there a policy for predicting and dealing with burn-out of staff?
11	Is there an agreed plan for transition to operations including parallel running of processes and technology?
12	Is there a single backlog of user requirements that is used to drive the activity and releases?
13	Have communications occurred, or been planned, to the wider organisational body to explain and prepare mindsets for the incremental delivery inherent in the agile approach?

5.4 External reviewer

Ref	Description
1	Do you fully understand the vision of the project? Can you describe the priority of benefits (and sub-benefits) and understand how these are delivered during the early projects/releases? Do you believe all the other reviewers understand likewise?
2	Do you understand the project roadmap that shows how both the business and technical work is structured into a series of incrementally delivered projects/product deliveries with clear definition of the early deliverables and outline definition of the later deliverables?
3	Do you believe that all the projects are coherent and 100 per cent focused on building one step at a time to the overall vision? Can you see evidence of how each release links to the target operating model? Can you see evidence that interfaces to other projects are understood and being actively managed?

(Continued)

Table 5.4 *Continued*

Ref	Description
4	Are the key stage or project deliverables defined by a milestone. Is delivery timeboxed and delivery dates held? Is there evidence that the business has been able to use the functionality of solutions delivered to date and subsequently been able to deliver expected benefits?
5	Is there evidence that the business and technical architecture is reviewed frequently, updated, communicated and revisions built into the later project/release definitions?
6	Is there evidence that post project/release lessons learned reviews have been carried out formally and lessons built into future projects/releases?
7	Is there an agreed plan for transition to operations including parallel running of processes and technology?
8	Is there a single backlog of user requirements that is used to drive the activity and releases?

Appendix A: References and further information

Agile Manifesto. Available at http://www.agilemanifesto.org/principles.html

APM Governance SIG (2007), *Co-Directing Change: A Guide to the Governance of Multi-Owned Projects*, Princes Risborough, Association for Project Management.

APM Governance SIG (2009), *Sponsoring Change: A Guide to the Governance Aspects of Project Sponsorship*, Princes Risborough, Association for Project Management.

APM Governance SIG (2011), *Directing Change: A Guide to the Governance of Project Management*, Princes Risborough, Association for Project Management.

Association for Project Management (2015), *Conditions for Project Success*. Available at https://www.apm.org.uk/conditions-for-project-success

Cabinet Office (2015), *Major Projects Authority assurance and approvals for agile delivery of digital services*. Available at https://www.gov.uk/government/uploads/system/uploads/attachment_data/file/444588/MPA_Guidance_Assuring_Agile_Projects.pdf

cPrime (2013), *Recipes for Agile Governance in the Enterprise*, The Enterprise Web

DSDM (n.d.) *AgileBA Agile Business Analysis*. Available at https://www.dsdm.org/shop/books/agile-business-analysis-agilebar-handbook

DSDM (n.d.) *AgilePgM Agile Programme Management*. Available at https://www.dsdm.org/shop/books/agile-programme-management-agilepgmr-handbook

DSDM (2014), *AgilePM Agile Project Framework*. Available at https://www.dsdm.org/shop/books/the-dsdm-agile-project-framework-handbook

OGC (2003) *Managing Successful Programmes*, London, The Stationery Office.

National Audit Office (2012), *Governance for Agile Delivery*. Available at https://www.nao.org.uk/wp-content/uploads/2012/07/governance_agile_delivery.pdf

PMI (2015), *Agile Certified Practitioner (PMI-ACP) Handbook*. Available at https://www.pmi.org/~/media/PDF/Certifications/handbooks/agile-certified-practitioner-handbook-acp.ashx

PRINCE2 Agile®. Available at https://www.axelos.com/best-practice-solutions/prince2/prince2-agile

Appendix B: Compendium of agile development methods

According to a recent survey by Arras People, 24 per cent of UK-based practitioners say they are using agile concepts in their day-to-day activities, yet only eight per cent have a recognised agile accreditation, mostly Scrum or AgilePM/DSDM. Other notable accreditations include PRINCE2 Agile® (AXELOS) and PMI-ACP (PMI). Other proprietary accreditations include DAD and SAFe.

Approaches also include DSDM Atern, eXtreme Programming (XP), Scrum and Lean. To put these agile approaches into context:

- AgilePM/DSDM from the not-for-profit DSDM Consortium (Dynamic Systems Development Method) is a long-established agile method, launched in 1995, that not only provides a framework at team level, but also includes feasibility study and architectural foundations. The method has evolved over the years and the popular AgilePM certifications are based on the latest version.
- XP (eXtreme Programming) focuses on IT development, allowing the programmers to decide the scope of deliveries, since the primary purpose of XP is incremental delivery. It is often combined with other agile approaches, which add-on the project and management elements. Examples of this would be XP with DSDM Atern and XP with Scrum.
- Scrum provides an excellent workface approach to allow work to be prioritised and delivered, using the concept of a constantly evolving backlog and absolute focus on timescale. Scrum is often paired with XP, and also often combined with DSDM Atern, where Scrum is used at the development team level, and DSDM Atern sits above the team to position the work within a project and to provide the project management elements.
- Lean is an approach that originated in the Toyota manufacturing environment in the 1940s. Lean drives work to be carried out in an efficient way through its main principle of 'eliminate waste'. In practice, this means avoiding anything that does not produce value for the customer. Lean is often used in conjunction with other agile approaches, e.g. Lean and DSDM Atern, Lean and Scrum, Lean and XP.